Water Slide Winner

Phil Kettle
illustrated by Craig Smith

Distributed in
the United States of America
by Pacific Learning
P.O. Box 2723
Huntington Beach, CA
92647-0723

Website:
www.pacificlearning.com

Published by Black Hills
(an imprint of Toocool Rules
Pty Ltd)
PO Box 2073
Fitzroy MDC VIC 3065
Australia
61+3+9419-9406

First published in the United States by Black Hills in 2004.
American editorial by Pacific Learning in 2004.
Text copyright © Phillip Kettle, 2003.
Illustration copyright © Toocool Rules Pty Limited, 2003.

 a black dog and Springhill book

Printed in China through Colorcraft Ltd, Hong Kong

ISBN 1 920924 14 0
PL-6213

10 9 8 7 6 5 4 3 2 1   08 07 06 05 04

Contents

Chapter 1
Hot!   **1**

Chapter 2
Toocool Water World   **6**

Chapter 3
The Water Slide   **11**

Chapter 4
Racing the Clock   **16**

Chapter 5
Slipping and Sliding   **22**

Toocool's Water Slide Glossary   29
Toocool's Map   30
Toocool's Quick Summary   32
The Toocool Water Slide   34
Q & A with Toocool   36
Water Slide Quiz   40

Toocool

Roberto

Marcy

Toocool's mom

Dog

Chapter 1

Hot!

It was summer vacation and it was hot. Really hot.

"I'm so hot my blood's boiling," said Roberto.

"I'm so hot my brain's sizzling," I said.

"Toocool, you don't have a brain," said Marcy.

Roberto, Marcy, Dog, and I were sitting under the lemon tree. It was the coolest place we could find.

"I wish I were at Wally's World," said Roberto.

"Actually, it's Wally's Water World," said Marcy. "It has three pools—and a whirlpool."

2

"Who cares about a whirlpool?" I said.

"It has a snack bar in the middle of one pool—with floating tables. The chairs float, too," said Roberto.

"Who cares about floating chairs?" I said.

"It has the longest water slide in the world," said Marcy.

"It did have the longest slide," I said.

"What?" asked Marcy.

"It did have the longest water slide in the world. That was before TWW—Toocool Water World!"

"Toocool, I think you do have a brain, and it's definitely sizzling!" said Marcy.

"You'll need to be nice to me if you want to visit Toocool Water World," I said.

"Toocool, I'd rather eat one of these sour lemons than be nice to you," said Marcy. "I'm going home."

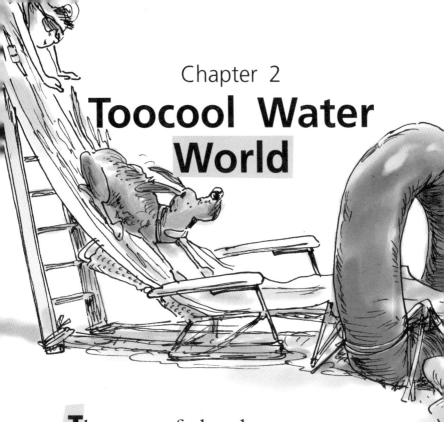

Chapter 2
Toocool Water World

The rest of the day was spent working on the incredible Toocool Water World.

Roberto, Dog, and I worked hard. Luckily, I had great ideas. I would probably be a water world designer if I weren't such an amazing athlete.

Marcy watched us from her backyard. We knew she was there because she kept throwing things at us.

"Only people who work on Toocool Water World get to use it," I told Roberto.

An orange flew over the fence and hit the garage wall.

"People who throw oranges can't enter the water slide race," said Roberto. "I'm going to set the world speed record for the water slide."

Another orange flew over.

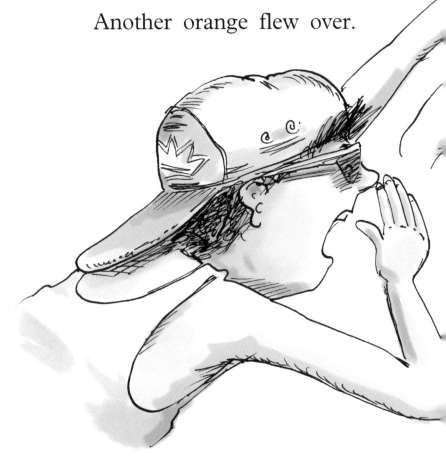

"You won't beat me," I said. "I'm going to be the water slide champion of the world."

"Toocool, you think you're the greatest at everything," yelled Marcy.

Marcy was right. I was great at most things. I just didn't like to brag about it.

That night, I dreamed I was sliding down the longest water slide in the world. It started from the top of a mountain. It was so high up, my head was in the clouds. The sign on the finish line read "Toocool Water World."

Chapter 3
The Water Slide

The next day was the great water slide race. Roberto came over early. We were going to squeeze in a few practice runs before the big event, but there was a problem.

"What happened to Toocool Water World?" said Roberto.

We were standing in the middle of TWW—or what was left of it.

"It was Marcy!" I said.

The TWW security guard, Dog, hadn't done his job.

The TWW manager stuck her head out of the kitchen window. She was a little bit grumpy.

"You boys left a big mess yesterday. I've cleaned up some of it. Now you clean up the rest... and put on some sunscreen!"

The manager hadn't been told about the building plans. I'd tell her after we finished rebuilding.

"Toocool, do you call that a water slide?" Marcy yelled from her tree house. "Maybe I should show you how to build one."

"Maybe you should," I said. Three workers were faster than two. Anyway, I knew I was in charge. I was the best water slide builder in the world.

14

By lunchtime, we'd built the biggest water slide ever. Roberto, Marcy, and I sat at the TWW snack bar and looked at our creation.

"Scared?" I asked them.

"Maybe you should be scared, Toocool," said Marcy. "Scared of me beating you."

I just smiled. Marcy would never be good enough to beat me at anything.

Chapter 4
Racing the Clock

The water slide had more bends and bumps than I could count. The winner would be the one to get down the slide in the least amount of time. I would go first.

"Why should you get to go first?" asked Roberto.

"It's Toocool Water World," I said. "I should go first."

My first time down the slide was a practice run. I had to get a feel for it.

I sat down and pushed off.
I was going really fast. Water
sprayed everywhere.

"Yes!" I said as I got to the
end. I punched the air.

It was Roberto's turn next. His run was okay, but he wasn't as fast as I was.

Then it was Marcy's turn. She shot along the slide at top speed. She was probably going as fast as she ever would, though.

This was only a practice run. Wait until I really put on some speed.

We spent the next few
hours training. We were getting
good, but we still hadn't timed
our slide runs. Marcy went
home to get her stopwatch.
Roberto went inside to get
a drink.

I looked at the sunscreen
bottle near the slide. It gave me
a great idea.

Marcy was sliding pretty
fast. I just needed an edge to
win—something to help me slip
through the water.

I grabbed the sunscreen and
rubbed it all over myself.

Chapter 5
Slipping and Sliding

When the others got back, we decided who would go first.

"I should go first," said Marcy, "because my name starts with *M*. *M* comes before *R* and *T*."

"Okay," I said. I wanted to go last anyway.

Roberto timed Marcy as she came down the slide.

"That was fast," said Roberto as he clicked the stopwatch. "Now stand back. I'm going to make that water boil."

Marcy timed Roberto.

"Not bad," said Marcy. "Still, not as fast as I was."

By now, a crowd had gathered. I was sure I saw people taking my picture.

I pushed off from the top of the slide. I sped through the water. I slid around the turns. I rode the bumps. The end was in sight.

"Wow!" said Marcy, as I raced past her.

"Toocool! Watch out!" yelled Roberto.

I passed the crowd of onlookers... and the security guard. I slid straight into the TWW snack bar.

Marcy said she was the winner. She had the fastest time. That's just because she didn't end up near the snack bar.

"Didn't I tell you to clean up this mess?" said the TWW manager.

It was time for Toocool Water World to close for the summer.

Actually, it was just as well that TWW closed. I had a summer job that would take up all my time. I bet I'll look great in my lifeguard uniform.

The End!

Toocool's
Water Slide Glossary

Designer—Someone who creates a sketch or plan for things like structures, gardens, or rooms.

Manager—A person who is in charge and makes sure no one breaks any rules.

Security guard—A person whose job is to protect a place from damage or theft.

Whirlpool—A bath or small pool that has heated water pumped into it.

Toocool's Map
Toocool Water World

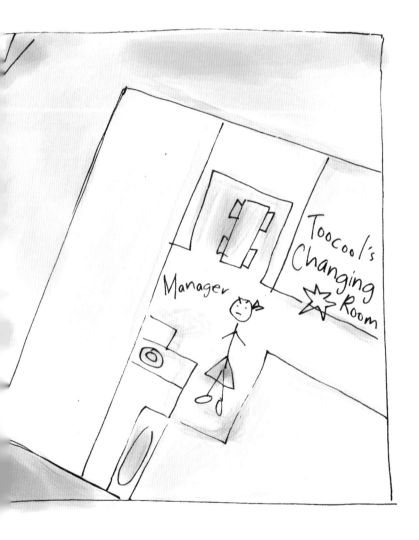

Manager

Toocool's
Changing
Room

Toocool's Quick Summary
Water Slides

Water slides are popular the world over with kids and adults—but especially with kids.

These fun slides can be found at water parks and pools. They can be built for indoor pools as well as outdoor pools. Some people, like me, can even make a water slide out of a plastic sheet for their own backyard.

Water slides can be open tubes or closed tubes. They can be wide enough for just one person to go down at a time or for a bunch of people.

Water slides can be straight and steep, or they can be very curvy.

Most water slides are made out of steel and fiberglass, but some water slides are created by nature. These slides are made naturally out of rock worn smooth by many years of water flowing over them.

Whatever kind of water slide it is, you know that Toocool will be the fastest slider of them all.

The **Toocool** Water Slide

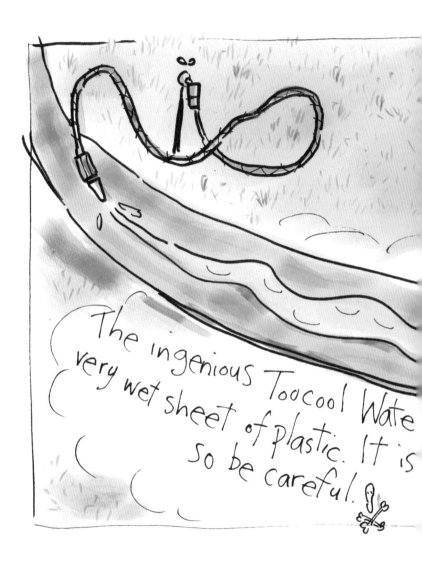

The ingenious Toocool Wate[r]
very wet sheet of plastic. It is
so be careful.

Slide uses a very long,
extremely slippery,

Q & A with Toocool
He Answers His Own Questions

Is water slide racing an Olympic sport?

Not yet, but with talent like mine, it won't be long before the world takes notice. Water slide racing would be a great sport to add to the next TWW Games. I have the perfect design for an eight-lane racing slide in my head. I'm sure I'll be the first person the Games Committee will contact.

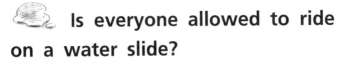 **Is everyone allowed to ride on a water slide?**

Almost anyone who is tall enough can go on a slide—even adults! If you're really young you probably should go on a water slide with an adult, no matter how tall you are. I never needed any help when I was younger. I'm a natural.

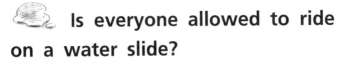 **Do you have advice for anyone who wants to go on a water slide?**

Wear lots of waterproof sunscreen. I use sunscreen to give me an edge over the other competitors. You should wear it anyway so you don't get sunburned. Don't forget to shout "Toocool rules" on your way down the water slide.

How long have you been interested in water slide design?

I've been interested ever since I spilled my milk on the kitchen floor and Dog slipped on it. He slid from one end of the kitchen to the other, then crashed into the garbage can. I thought it looked like fun, except for the crashing part. I want to build water slides that connect countries because I think that would be a great way to travel.

What is the longest water slide in the world?

The water slide in Toocool Water World. Well, it was the longest. It was closed down after complaints from management.

What makes a great water slide?

A great water slide should be fast and unpredictable—like me. It could have lots of curves or big drops. It could be in a tunnel, so you can't see where you're going. That scares a lot of people. Of course, it doesn't scare me.

What is your favorite kind of water slide for racing?

If I'm racing, I like a slide that goes straight down. I don't want any twists or turns to slow me down.

Water Slide Quiz
How Much Do You Know about Water Slides?

Q1 What are many water slides made from?

A. Plastic. **B.** Glass. **C.** Steel and fiberglass.

Q2 What do the letters *TWW* stand for?

A. Toocool Will Win. **B.** Toocool Water World. **C.** That Won't Work.

Q3 What should you wear when you go water sliding?
A. Swimsuit. **B.** Football gear.
C. Pajamas.

Q4 What shape is the fastest water slide ride?
A. Round. **B.** Straight. **C.** Curvy and bumpy.

Q5 Who is the security guard at TWW?
A. Dog. **B.** Mr. Lopez. **C.** Bert the Rooster.

Q6 Why does Toocool wear sunscreen when water sliding?
A. To look good. **B.** To scare the competition. **C.** To help him slip along the slide faster.

Q7 What is a stopwatch?

A. A watch that doesn't work.

B. A watch used to time a race.

C. When you stop looking at something.

 Q8 Whose name comes first in the alphabet?

A. Marcy. *B.* Toocool. *C.* Roberto.

 Q9 Where might you find a water slide?

A. In your bedroom.

B. At a movie theater.

C. At an amusement park.

 Q10 Who is the best water slider in the world?

A. Toocool. *B.* Marcy. *C.* Roberto.

ANSWERS

🐢 *1* C. 🐢 *2* B. 🐢 *3* A.

🐢 *4* B. 🐢 *5* A. 🐢 *6* C.

🐢 *7* B. 🐢 *8* A. 🐢 *9* C.

🐢 *10* A.

If you got ten questions right, Toocool would like to race you when TWW reopens. If you got more than five right, you can compete against Roberto. If you got fewer than five right, you should probably stick to the baby slides.

Beach Patrol

It's just another beach patrol for **Toocool** lifeguard—or is it? What happens when a deep-sea creature stalks Marcy? Can **Toocool** save the day?

Titles in the Toocool series

Slam Dunk Magician

Fishing Fanatic

BMX Champ

Surfing Pro

Tennis Ace

Skateboard Standout

Golfing Giant

Football Legend

Sonic Mountain Bike

Supreme Sailor

Gocart Genius

Invincible Iron Man

Soccer Superstar

Baseball's Best

Water Slide Winner

Beach Patrol

Rodeo Cowboy

Space Captain

Daredevil on Ice

Discus Dynamo